BREAKING
FREE
SURVIVING FROM CHILDHOOD
TRAUMA

BENJAMIN HOLLAND

Ordering Information:

Prime Seven Media
518 Landmann St.
Tomah City, WI 54660

Printed in the United States of America

In the dimming light of a childhood loss, Lies the shattered remnants of innocence tossed.

In the echoing silence of secrets untold, My god my god the fear and the Lies the pain of a story too heavy to hold.

Tiny hearts once filled with laughter and glee, Now bear the weight of what no child should see. They're so innocent and sometimes unaware and the Innocent eyes, that were once so bright with hope and trust, Now carry the scars of betrayal and unjust.

The echoes of fear still linger in the air, A haunting reminder of a Little one's life can be so unfair.

The wounds run deep, unseen by the naked eye, A silent scream that no one can hear but me.

Amidst the darkness, a flicker of light, A glimmer of strength, a will to take on the flight.

For though the past may cast a long, dark shade, In the dawn of healing, a new path is laid.

So let the broken pieces find their mend, Let the wounded heart learn to love and transcend.

For in the journey from darkness to light, Lies the power to reclaim and rewrite. And in those little one's eyes, they'll know everything will be all right.

This poem attempts to capture the pain and lasting impact of childhood trauma and abuse, while also emphasizing the resilience and hope for healing and recovery. With that said I hope this poem provides a means for survivors of childhood trauma.

Now I want to talk about my childhood trauma:

My sister and I were tortured by my parents they used to tie a rope around our ankles when we were butt naked pull it over the door and shut the door so the rope wouldn't slip and they would beat us upside down I remember I used to tell my sister to pretend as you fainted that's the only way they would stop, and then there were times when we were sleeping and I remember feeling pain when I was asleep I didn't realize what it was and my mother was beating us with a stick while we were sleeping and when we got up and ran underneath the bed she with the ammonia under the bed to smoke us out and when we came out the beatings continued and then there was much more… I remember one time my mother kept telling My sister all day long that she was going to throw a pot of hot water on her but I didn't know if she was really going to do it and mother came home her and my sister are in the kitchen and I hear My sister scream I scream like I never heard before and when I went into the kitchen it happened I saw My sister skin peeling off of her and she was still screaming and I didn't know what to do and I remember my mother was telling her once the ambulance got there that it was an accident but I knew it wasn't an accident and then there was another time I came home and My sister looked like she was in a fight with Mike Tyson and she said my mother did it because I asked her what happened and my mother hit her with a cast iron skillet that day my sister died but she said when she was out she saw a light and it was God and he told her to go back I'm not ready for you those or just a few torture items that My sister and I went through so when I talk about the pain and the trauma of childhood trauma I lived it... so you see in order for me to survive I for gave my mother my father and my grandmother but my sister is still broken because she never got help so in that regard it's very important to get help as soon as possible are those demons will eat you from the inside out for the rest of your life that's why so many people out there that are on drugs alcohol or converting mental health issues to this day because they never addressed it I did and that's why I want to write about it.

"Breaking Free: Healing from Childhood Trauma" offers a roadmap for individuals who are ready to embark on a journey of healing, growth, and transformation. Remember, healing from childhood trauma takes time and effort, but with the right tools, support, and mindset, you can break free from the chains of your past and create a brighter, more fulfilling future. You deserve to live a life of joy, resilience, and well-being.

After breaking free from childhood trauma one of the first things is to forgive. That's what I did because for years after I kept having these catastrophic dreams of fighting with my mother so after I forgave her, they stopped. That's what I'm trying to explain they were knockdown drag-out fights, and I would wake up and cold sweats, so I had to find a way to stop it all and mass when forgiveness came into play in my life. Forgiveness can be a powerful step in the healing process after experiencing childhood trauma, but it's important to note that forgiveness is a personal choice and not a requirement for healing. Different individuals may have different perspectives on forgiveness based on their unique experiences and circumstances.

Here are a few points to consider:

Acknowledging and processing emotions:

Before forgiveness can be considered, it's crucial to allow yourself to acknowledge and process the emotions associated with the trauma. This includes anger, sadness, fear, and any other emotions that may arise. Giving yourself permission to feel and express these emotions can be an essential part of the healing journey.

Understanding forgiveness:

Forgiveness is not about condoning or forgetting what happened. It does not mean that you have to reconcile with the person who caused the trauma or that you have to minimize the impact of the experience. Instead, forgiveness is a personal choice to release the emotional burden and find inner peace. It is a process of letting go and moving forward, focusing on your well-being rather than seeking revenge or holding onto resentment.

Timing and readiness:

Forgiveness is a deeply personal decision, and it may not be appropriate or possible immediately after the trauma. It takes time to heal, and everyone's healing journey is unique. Rushing the process of forgiveness can be counterproductive and hinder the healing process. It's important to be patient with yourself and allow the necessary time to heal before considering forgiveness.

Seeking professional support:

Working with a therapist or counselor who specializes in trauma can be immensely beneficial in navigating the healing process. They can provide guidance, support, and tools to help you work through the trauma, including exploring forgiveness if and when you're ready. Ultimately, forgiveness is a personal choice, and there is no right or wrong timeline for it. It's important to prioritize your well-being and focus on the healing process in a way that feels right for you, that's the reason why I started seeking professional help when I was writing my first book because it was so emotional I used to have to stop and go see a counselor with regards to the feelings that I was having because it seems like everything was coming back all over again. You see a lot of people write about childhood trauma or trauma in general but unless you lived it you won't understand it just saying... I still have nightmares today about the trauma that I went through as a child it will never go away but you can learn to live with it.

Understanding childhood without neutering from their mother.

The development and upbringing of a child without the presence or involvement of their mother. While it is ideal for children to have both parents actively involved in their lives, there are situations where children grow up without their mother due to various circumstances, such as separation, divorce, death, or other reasons.

It is important to note that every child's experience will be unique and influenced by several factors, including their age, personality, the quality of the relationship with their mother, the support system available to them, and the circumstances surrounding the mother's absence.

Here are some key points to consider when understanding childhood without the presence of a mother:

1. Role of other caregivers: In the absence of the mother, other caregivers, such as fathers, grandparents, relatives, or close family friends, may step in to provide care, guidance, and emotional support to the child. These individuals can play crucial roles in the child's development and create a nurturing environment.

2. Emotional impact: The absence of a mother can have emotional implications for a child. They may experience feelings of loss, sadness, or abandonment. Caregivers need to address these emotions and provide a safe space for the child to express their feelings.

3. Gender-specific needs: Mothers often play a unique role in a child's life, particularly when it comes to meeting gender-specific needs. In the case of a mother's absence, other caregivers can help fill this gap by providing appropriate guidance and support based on the child's gender.

4. Building a support network: Surrounding the child with a strong support network can help mitigate the challenges associated with the absence of a mother. This network can include family members, friends, teachers, counselors, or support groups, who can provide guidance, love, and stability.

5. Open communication and honesty: Caregivers need to maintain open and honest communication with the child about their mother's absence, particularly as the child grows older and begins to understand the situation. Age-appropriate discussions can help the child process their emotions and develop a sense of understanding.

While the absence of a mother can present challenges, children have shown remarkable resilience in adapting to different family structures. With love, support, and a nurturing environment, children can still thrive and develop into well-adjusted individuals.

What happens when men do not get nurturing from their mothers and they meet a woman that nurtures them?

When men do not receive nurturing from their mothers during their upbringing and subsequently meet a woman who provides them with nurturing, several possible scenarios and outcomes can occur:

1. Emotional Healing: The nurturing presence of a woman can have a healing effect on men who lack maternal nurturing. It can help them address unresolved emotional wounds, develop a sense of security, and experience the love and care they may have missed during their earlier years. This emotional healing process can contribute to their overall well-being and personal growth.

2. Attachment and Bonding: Men who lack maternal nurturing may feel a strong attachment and bonding with a woman who provides them with care and nurturance. They may develop a deep emotional connection and rely on her for emotional support and comfort. This attachment can be similar to the bond one might have with a mother figure.

3. Trust and Security: The presence of a nurturing woman can help men build trust and feel emotionally secure. When they experience consistent care and support, it can positively impact their ability to form healthy relationships, build trust in others, and develop a sense of emotional security that was lacking before.

4. Positive Relationship Patterns: Men who did not receive nurturing from their mothers may have difficulties with intimacy, trust, and emotional expression in relationships. However, when they encounter a nurturing woman, they have an opportunity to learn positive relationship patterns. They can observe and experience healthy behaviors, communication, and emotional support, which can help

them develop more satisfying and fulfilling relationships in the future.

5. Emotional Dependency: In some cases, men who lack maternal nurturing may become emotionally dependent on the woman who nurtures them. They may rely heavily on her for emotional validation, support, and decision-making. While receiving nurturing is beneficial, individuals need to develop their own emotional resilience and self-care practices to avoid becoming overly reliant on others for their emotional well-being.

It's important to note that individual experiences may vary, and not all men will respond to nurturing in the same way. Some men may be more receptive and open to accepting nurturing, while others may initially struggle with trust or have difficulty embracing vulnerability. Professional therapy or counseling can be beneficial for individuals who have experienced significant emotional neglect or trauma and require additional support in navigating these issues.

This is my perspective for a child I don't believe in beating or hitting a child ... because they're little people with little personalities I think you can have a conversation.

Concerning the many people who share the belief that physical punishment, such as beating or hitting, is not an effective or appropriate way to discipline a child. Instead, they advocate for alternative approaches that focus on communication, understanding, and teaching appropriate behavior.

Having a conversation with a child can be a constructive way to address their behavior and help them understand the consequences of their actions. It allows for open dialogue, mutual respect, and an opportunity to guide them towards making better choices.

Communication can also help foster a strong parent-child relationship built on trust and understanding.

Various positive discipline techniques can be used instead of physical punishment. These include setting clear expectations, offering praise and rewards for good behavior, establishing consistent routines and boundaries, using time-outs or temporary removal of privileges, and teaching problem-solving skills. It's important to remember that each child is unique, and what works for one may not work for another, so it's essential to tailor discipline strategies to the individual child.

It's worth noting that many countries and legal systems have recognized the potential harm of physical punishment and have implemented laws or guidelines to protect children from physical abuse. These laws aim to promote non-violent methods of discipline and ensure the well-being of children.

Ultimately, the goal of discipline should be to teach children self-discipline, empathy, and respect for others, rather than instilling fear or causing harm. There's more to come this one's gonna be a long one!!!

How to fix a man or a woman after childhood trauma to break them from being abusive in a toxic relationship.

Addressing the impact of childhood trauma and breaking the cycle of abuse in a toxic relationship is a complex process that typically requires professional help. While I can provide some general guidance, it's important to note that every individual and situation is unique and personalized therapy is often necessary. Here are some steps that may be helpful:

1. Encourage self-awareness: Help the individual recognize the impact of their childhood trauma on their behavior and the patterns that contribute to their toxic relationship. This can

be done through open and non-judgmental conversations, where you express concern for their well-being.

2. Encourage therapy: Suggest that the person seek professional help from a therapist experienced in trauma and relationship issues. Therapy can provide a safe space for them to explore their past, understand the root causes of their behavior, and develop healthier coping strategies.

3. Promote self-care: Encourage the person to engage in self-care activities that promote their physical, emotional, and mental well-being. This can include regular exercise, healthy eating, pursuing hobbies, and practicing relaxation techniques such as meditation or deep breathing exercises.

4. Develop healthy coping mechanisms: Help the person identify and develop healthier coping mechanisms to replace abusive behaviors. This may involve teaching them skills such as effective communication, conflict resolution, anger management, and stress reduction techniques.

5. Encourage support networks: Encourage the individual to build a support network of friends, family, or support groups where they can find understanding, empathy, and guidance. Supportive relationships can provide a sense of belonging and help them feel less isolated.

6. Build self-esteem and self-worth: Childhood trauma can erode self-esteem and self-worth. Help the person recognize and celebrate their strengths, talents, and achievements. Encourage them to engage in activities that promote self-confidence and personal growth.

7. Set boundaries: Teach the person the importance of setting healthy boundaries in relationships. This includes

recognizing their limits and communicating with them assertively, as well as respecting the boundaries of others.

8. Patience and compassion: Supporting someone in their journey of healing and overcoming abusive behaviors requires patience and compassion. Remember that change takes time, and it's important to avoid blaming or shaming them for past actions.

It's crucial to involve professionals, such as therapists or counselors, who can provide the necessary expertise and guidance throughout the healing process.

I decided to be celibate to be able to understand a relationship because I had so many so in that regard I just decided to be celibate and fix myself first before I got into another relationship and what I found is in my mind I felt so much better because until you fix yourself and then you get into another relationship and you bring it all baggage into the new relationship it'll never work out because both parties are broken and the cycle has not broken so everybody's broken you feel me, in that regard, I would suggest everyone explore their relationships and figure out where their head is because society says that a man and a woman has to be together or a woman Hass to have a man and a man have to have a woman that's not true I've been celibate for four years and the love that I have in my heart is with my children it's not for a woman because I had to fix myself and I'm still fixing myself because I was broken for so very long with regards to childhood trauma, etc. after facing childhood trauma as an adolescent, the coping mechanism when you are an adult.

I can provide some general information on coping mechanisms for adults who have experienced childhood trauma. It's important to note that seeking professional help from a therapist or counselor is highly recommended to address and work through trauma effectively. Here are a few coping strategies that some individuals find helpful:

1. Therapy and Counseling: Engaging in therapy or counseling with a trained professional who specializes in trauma can provide valuable support and guidance. Therapies such as cognitive-behavioral therapy (CBT), eye movement desensitization and reprocessing (EMDR), or dialectical behavior therapy (DBT) may help address trauma-related symptoms.

2. Self-Care: Taking care of yourself physically, emotionally, and mentally is crucial. This can include activities such as regular exercise, proper nutrition, sufficient sleep, engaging in hobbies, practicing mindfulness or meditation, and setting boundaries to maintain a healthy work-life balance.

3. Supportive Relationships: Surrounding yourself with supportive and understanding individuals can make a significant difference. Building and maintaining healthy relationships with friends, family, or support groups can provide a sense of validation, empathy, and connection.

4. Expressive Therapies: Engaging in creative outlets like art therapy, music therapy, or writing can help individuals express and process their emotions in a non-verbal way. These forms of therapy can be particularly effective for individuals who find it challenging to communicate their feelings verbally.

5. Mindfulness and Relaxation Techniques: Learning and practicing relaxation techniques such as deep breathing exercises, progressive muscle relaxation, or guided imagery

can help manage anxiety and stress associated with trauma triggers.

6   Education and Knowledge: Educating yourself about trauma and its effects can help you understand your experiences and develop a sense of empowerment. Reading books, and articles, or attending trauma workshops can provide valuable insights and coping strategies.

7   Healthy Lifestyle Choices: Engaging in activities that promote overall well-being, such as regular exercise, a balanced diet, and avoiding substance abuse, can support your mental and emotional resilience.

Coping mechanisms can vary from person to person, and what works for one individual may not work for another. It's essential to find coping strategies that resonate with you and seek professional help to guide you through the healing process.

Following these steps regarding childhood trauma will help you survive the rest of your life.

Addressing childhood trauma can have a significant impact on an individual's overall well-being and ability to navigate life successfully. While every person's journey is unique, certain steps can generally contribute to healing and resilience. Here are some suggestions:

1. Acknowledge and understand the trauma: Recognize that you have experienced childhood trauma and understand its impact on your life. Educate yourself about trauma and its effects to gain insights into your experiences and reactions.

2. Seek professional help: Consider working with a qualified therapist or counselor who specializes in trauma. Therapy

can provide a safe space to explore your emotions, develop coping strategies, and facilitate healing.

3. Build a support system: Surround yourself with a supportive network of friends, family, or support groups who can offer empathy, understanding, and encouragement. Sharing your experiences with trusted individuals can help alleviate feelings of isolation and provide validation.

4. Practice self-care: Prioritize self-care activities that promote your physical, mental, and emotional well-being. Engage in activities such as exercise, mindfulness, hobbies, and relaxation techniques that help you manage stress and enhance your overall resilience.

5. Develop coping mechanisms: Explore and adopt healthy coping strategies to manage triggers and emotional distress. This may include deep breathing exercises, journaling, practicing mindfulness, or seeking creative outlets like art or music.

6. Process and express emotions: Allow yourself to express and process your emotions related to the trauma. This can be done through therapy, journaling, art, or talking to a trusted friend. Validating and understanding your emotions can support healing and prevent them from being suppressed or manifesting negatively.

7. Establish healthy boundaries: Set and enforce healthy boundaries in your relationships and interactions. Learn to recognize and prioritize your needs and communicate assertively when necessary.

8. Develop resilience and self-compassion: Cultivate resilience by focusing on your strengths and building your capacity

to bounce back from challenges. Practice self-compassion, treating yourself with kindness, understanding, and patience throughout your healing journey.

9. Consider support groups or specialized programs: Joining support groups or participating in specialized programs for individuals who have experienced childhood trauma can provide additional resources, validation, and opportunities for growth.

Remember, healing from childhood trauma is a deeply personal process that takes time and effort. It's essential to consult with a mental health professional who can provide personalized guidance based on your specific circumstances and needs.

After surviving childhood trauma as an adolescent, you're an adult in a relationship how to break the cycle and not bring that into your adult relationship?

Breaking the cycle of childhood trauma and ensuring it doesn't negatively impact your adult relationships is a courageous and important endeavor. Here are some steps you can take to help you on this journey:

1. Seek professional help: Consider working with a therapist or counselor who specializes in trauma and relationships. They can help you explore and process your childhood trauma, understand its effects on your adult relationships, and develop healthy coping strategies.

2. Educate yourself about healthy relationships: Learn about what constitutes a healthy relationship, including aspects such as effective communication, boundaries, trust, and mutual respect. Books, online resources, and workshops can provide valuable insights and guidance.

3. Practice self-awareness: Cultivate self-awareness to recognize how your childhood trauma may be influencing your thoughts, feelings, and behaviors in your adult relationship. Pay attention to your triggers, emotional reactions, and patterns that may stem from your past. Mindfulness exercises and journaling can be helpful in this regard.

4. Communicate openly with your partner: Share your experiences and concerns with your partner. Open communication builds trust and allows both of you to understand each other better. Explain how your childhood trauma may affect your behavior at times, so they can support you appropriately.

5. Establish healthy boundaries: Set clear boundaries in your relationship. Understand your needs and communicate them effectively. Respect your partner's boundaries as well. This creates a safe space for both of you and helps establish a foundation of trust.

6. Practice self-care: Prioritize self-care activities that promote your emotional and mental well-being. Engage in activities that make you feel good, reduce stress, and promote relaxation. This may include exercise, hobbies, spending time with loved ones, or practicing self-compassion.

7. Challenge negative beliefs: Childhood trauma can lead to negative beliefs about oneself and relationships. Challenge and reframe those beliefs. Recognize that you are not defined by your past and that you are capable of forming healthy, fulfilling relationships.

8. Develop healthy coping strategies: Identify healthy coping mechanisms to manage stress, anxiety, or triggers that

may arise during your relationship. This could include deep breathing exercises, mindfulness techniques, seeking support from friends, or engaging in creative outlets.

9. Practice forgiveness and let go of the past: Forgiving those who caused the childhood trauma, as well as forgiving yourself for any perceived shortcomings, can be a powerful step toward healing. Letting go of the past allows you to focus on the present and future of your relationship.

Breaking the cycle of childhood trauma takes time and effort. Be patient and kind to yourself throughout the process. Celebrate your progress and seek support when needed. With dedication and self-reflection, you can build a healthy and fulfilling adult relationship.

How to forgive the people who traumatized you as a child and now you're an adult.

Forgiving the people who traumatized you as a child can be a difficult and complex process, but it is possible with time and effort. Here are some steps you can take to work towards forgiveness:

Let's take a trip down memory lane I remember when I for gave my mother she was on her dying bed I was a very popular DJ in Seattle Washington I remember when I heard she was dying I knew I had to go see her but it wasn't only for forgiving her I just wanted closure and I remember going into the room and she was on her bed and she looked really bad and all I ask her was why did you do the things that you did to my sister and I and all she did was look me in the face she wouldn't even answer and I remember walking out the room I remember my grandmother was sitting on the couch in the living room and I asked her what did you do to my mother to make her the most and that she was she wouldn't answer and I walked out House never to return back to my DJ gig until a week later fact House and

I started crying in the DJ booth and I couldn't figure out why and I couldn't stop crying but I realize that I was still broken but I Had forgiven them because the more I kept that inside of me it was going to eat me from the inside out and I realize that that point that I didn't need closure I needed to forgive.

1. Acknowledge your pain: Recognize and validate the pain and trauma you experienced as a child. Understand that your feelings are valid and it's okay to be angry, hurt, or resentful.

2. Understand the impact: Educate yourself about the effects of trauma and how it can shape your thoughts, emotions, and behavior. This understanding can help you develop empathy and compassion for yourself.

3. Seek support: Consider seeking professional help from a therapist, counselor, or support group specializing in trauma. They can provide guidance, a safe space to express your emotions, and strategies to cope with your past experiences.

4. Practice self-care: Engage in activities that promote self-care and healing, such as exercise, mindfulness, meditation, journaling, or creative outlets. Take care of your physical, emotional, and mental well-being.

5. Set boundaries: Establish healthy boundaries with the people who have caused you harm. This may involve limiting or cutting off contact with them, particularly if they continue to be toxic or abusive. Prioritize your well-being and surround yourself with supportive and caring people.

6. Practice empathy and perspective-taking: Try to understand the people who hurt you from a broader perspective.

Consider their own life experiences, struggles, and potential factors that may have contributed to their behavior. This does not excuse their actions but helps you develop empathy and see them as flawed human beings.

7. Challenge negative beliefs: Examine any negative beliefs or self-blame you may have internalized as a result of the trauma. Replace them with more positive and realistic beliefs about yourself and your worth.

8. Let go of resentment: Understand that holding onto anger and resentment only continues to hurt you. Forgiveness is a process that involves letting go of negative emotions and finding peace within yourself. It does not mean condoning or forgetting what happened, but rather freeing yourself from the burden of carrying the pain.

9. Write a letter (optional): Consider writing a letter to the person who traumatized you, expressing your feelings and thoughts. You do not necessarily have to send it; it can be a therapeutic exercise to release your emotions and gain closure.

10. Be patient with yourself: Healing and forgiveness take time. It's normal to have setbacks and moments of anger or sadness. Be patient and kind to yourself throughout the process and remember that forgiveness is a personal journey unique to each individual.

Forgiveness is not an obligation, and it may not be the right path for everyone. It's a personal choice that depends on your healing journey and what feels right for you.

Suffering through childhood trauma and will infect you and your children.

That's the reason why I never had any biological children because I was afraid was the cycle broken or was it not broken I wasn't sure so I chose not.

Childhood trauma can have a profound impact on a person's life, and it's important to seek professional help and support to heal and cope with the effects of trauma.

It's important to note that trauma itself is not contagious. It's an individual experience that affects the person who has gone through it. However, trauma can have ripple effects on relationships and family dynamics. If a person who has experienced trauma is not receiving the necessary support and treatment, it can potentially affect their interactions with others, including their children.

If you or someone you know is dealing with the effects of childhood trauma, I strongly encourage reaching out to a mental health professional or a counselor who can provide guidance and support. They can help you navigate the healing process, develop coping mechanisms, and address any concerns you may have about the impact on your children.

You don't have to face this alone, and there are resources available to help you and your family through difficult times.

They never gave us a manual on how to be a parent.

I know there is no official manual or set of instructions that can fully prepare someone for the experience of being a parent. Parenting is a complex and dynamic role that requires a combination of knowledge, skills, and personal intuition. While there are many resources available such as books, classes, and online communities that can provide guidance and support, every child and every family is unique, and what works for one may not work for another.

Parenting is often a learning process where you adapt and grow alongside your child. It's normal to encounter challenges and make mistakes along the way. It's important to remember that no one is a perfect parent, and it's okay to seek help and advice from others when needed.

Here are a few general principles that may help you navigate the journey of parenting:

1. Love and nurture your child: Show your child love, affection, and support. Create a nurturing and safe environment where they can grow and develop.

2. Be patient: Children go through different stages of development, and they may test your patience at times. Try to remain calm and understand that their behavior is often a result of their stage of development.

3. Communicate effectively: Establish open lines of communication with your child from an early age. Listen to them, validate their feelings, and encourage them to express themselves. Effective communication helps build trust and strengthens your relationship.

4. Set clear boundaries and expectations: Children thrive with structure and consistency. Establish clear rules and expectations and enforce them consistently. This helps children feel secure and understand what is expected of them.

5. Practice self-care: Parenting can be demanding and exhausting. Take care of yourself physically, mentally, and emotionally. Seek support from your partner, family, or friends, and make time for activities that recharge and rejuvenate you.

6. Seek knowledge and support: Educate yourself about child development, parenting techniques, and strategies for handling common challenges. Join parenting groups or seek guidance from trusted professionals when needed.

That parenting is a journey, and you will continue to learn and grow as you go along. Trust yourself, rely on your instincts, and be open to adapting your approach as your child's needs change over time.

Open communication and transparency with your children are very important.

Open communication and transparency with your children are essential for building trust, fostering healthy relationships, and promoting their emotional well-being. When parents create an environment of open communication, it allows children to feel comfortable expressing their thoughts, feelings, and concerns without fear of judgment or punishment. Here are some key aspects to consider:

1. Active Listening: Give your children your undivided attention when they want to talk. Maintain eye contact, show genuine interest, and avoid interrupting or rushing them. By actively listening, you demonstrate that their thoughts and feelings are important to you.

2. Create a Safe Space: Establish an atmosphere of acceptance and non-judgment. Encourage open dialogue by letting your children know that they can talk to you about anything and that you are there to support and guide them.

3. Be Available: Make yourself available for conversations and encourage your children to approach you whenever they need to talk. This includes being accessible both physically and emotionally. Be mindful of their cues and initiate

conversations when you sense something might be on their minds.

4. Respect Their Feelings: Validate your children's emotions and let them know that it's okay to feel a certain way. Avoid dismissing or belittling their feelings, as this can discourage them from being open with you in the future.

5. Age-Appropriate Communication: Tailor your communication to the age and maturity level of your children. Use language and explanations that they can understand. As they grow older, you can gradually introduce more complex topics and engage in deeper discussions.

6. Be Honest and Authentic: Encourage honesty by modeling it yourself. If your children ask you questions, answer truthfully in an age-appropriate manner. If you don't know the answer, admit it, and offer to find out together. Avoid manipulating or withholding information that is important for their understanding or well-being.

7. Set Boundaries and Expectations: While promoting open communication, it's also important to establish boundaries and expectations. Teach your children about respectful communication and the importance of listening to others. Ensure they understand that honesty should be balanced with kindness and empathy.

8. Problem-Solving and Conflict Resolution: Encourage your children to express their thoughts and concerns when conflicts arise. Teach them problem-solving skills and guide them in finding constructive solutions. This helps build their confidence in navigating difficult situations.

Remember, open communication and transparency should be a continuous effort. It may take time for children to feel comfortable opening up, so be patient and persistent. By fostering a culture of trust and open dialogue, you can strengthen your relationship with your children and support their emotional development.

I truly believe that parents should start giving their children responsibility at a very young age to prepare them for life, in general, a lot of parents out there or not getting their kids ready for that world out there, and then when they're out there on their own they don't know how to survive to start giving the kids responsibilities at a very young age pay them to take the garbage out Pam to clean up the room just paid them to do whatever needs to be done around the house so they can understand the responsibility and they're getting compensated for the chores that get them ready for the work environment and it also teaches them responsibility.

It is very important to praise your child for their good deeds, whether it's related to schoolwork or chores. Praise and recognition play a crucial role in a child's development and can have a positive impact on their self-esteem, motivation, and overall well-being. Here are a few reasons why praising your child for their accomplishments and good behavior is beneficial:

1. Positive reinforcement: Praising your child reinforces positive behavior and encourages them to continue their efforts. When children receive praise, they feel acknowledged and valued, which motivates them to repeat the behavior that earned them the praise in the first place.

2. Boosts self-esteem: Genuine praise helps build a child's self-esteem by highlighting their strengths and abilities. When children feel good about themselves and their

accomplishments, they develop a positive self-image and are more likely to take on new challenges with confidence.

3. Encourages a growth mindset: Praising your child's efforts and progress, rather than solely focusing on outcomes, promotes a growth mindset. By emphasizing the process of learning and improvement, you teach your child that their abilities can be developed through hard work and perseverance. This mindset fosters resilience and a willingness to take on challenges.

4. Reinforces values and character: Praising your child's good deeds helps reinforce positive values and character traits. When you acknowledge their efforts in completing chores or being responsible, you're teaching them the importance of responsibility, diligence, and contributing to the household.

However, it's important to provide praise effectively. Here are a few tips:

- Be specific: Instead of generic praise, provide specific feedback that highlights what your child did well. This helps them understand exactly what behavior or action is being acknowledged.

- Be genuine: Children can often sense when praise is insincere. Offer genuine praise that reflects your true appreciation for their efforts.

- Balance praise with constructive feedback: While it's crucial to praise your child, it's also important to provide constructive feedback when necessary. This helps them understand areas for improvement and provides an opportunity for growth.

The goal is to create a balanced approach where praise is given when deserved, but not overused or given for every single action. This helps children develop a healthy understanding of their achievements and fosters intrinsic motivation.

I remember the only time my mother gave me any kind of praise was when I was in college but the only reason why she was doing that was that she was taking Social Security money from my father because my father's Social Security will pay for my tuition but all she wanted was the information so she can have my brother pretend like he was me and she got all that money the state paid for my education ain't that some shit

I can never remember one time when my mom hugged me and told me that she loved me I can't even remember a time when she hugged me the only times I remembered was when we were getting high together that's it and that's when she showed the most love can you imagine.

As it relates to childhood trauma I remember my sister she loved school but her punishment for my mother was not to let her go to school and that broke her it broke her and she stayed with the other children and suffered and she's still suffering today and she broke today because she never forgave that's why I say it's very important to forgive I remember one time when I went home and my sister look like she was in a fight with Mike Tyson and I asked what happened to you and she said mommy did it she hit it with a cast-iron skillet and I told my sister if we don't leave now she's gonna kill us and she wants to stay and she did stay I left sometimes I feel like I was a coward because I left her there but I knew if I didn't leave when I left there was gonna be consequences and I'd always had an exit plan from the time I was nine years old I was just waiting for it.

But I know now I have a son he's not my biological son but I've been there with him from day one and I love him more than I love myself and I know now the cycle is broken and I want to give him all the love and nurturing that I never had because I was traumatized as a child but now I'm unbroken and I'm well because I forgave my mother.

How to Raticate the demons that are inside you when you don't forgive.

Dealing with inner demons and finding forgiveness can be a challenging and deeply personal journey. While I'm not a mental health professional, I can offer some general suggestions that may help you in your process. It's important to note that seeking the guidance of a qualified therapist or counselor can provide you with the personalized support you may need. Here are a few steps you can consider:

1. Acknowledge and accept your emotions: Recognize and accept the emotions that arise within you, such as anger, resentment, or fear. It's essential to acknowledge these feelings without judgment.

2. Understand the impact of holding onto grudges: Reflect on the negative effects that holding onto unforgiveness can have on your well-being. It can lead to increased stress, anxiety, and even physical health issues. Understanding these consequences can motivate you to seek forgiveness.

3. Cultivate self-compassion: Treat yourself with kindness and compassion. Remember that everyone makes mistakes, including yourself. Practice self-forgiveness and recognize that you are human and capable of growth.

4. Shift your perspective: Try to see the situation from different angles. Consider the perspective of the person you're struggling to forgive and try to understand their motivations or circumstances. This doesn't justify their actions but can help you develop empathy and see the bigger picture.

5. Practice empathy and compassion: Put yourself in the other person's shoes and try to understand their emotions and struggles. Recognize that forgiveness is not condoning their actions but rather freeing yourself from the burden of resentment.

6. Release negative emotions: Find healthy ways to release negative emotions, such as through journaling, talking to a trusted friend or therapist, practicing mindfulness or meditation, or engaging in physical activities like exercise or yoga.

7. Set boundaries: Forgiveness does not mean forgetting or allowing yourself to be continually hurt. Establishing healthy boundaries can protect your well-being while still working towards forgiveness.

8. Seek support: Consider reaching out to a therapist or counselor who can provide guidance and support throughout your forgiveness journey. They can help you explore your emotions, work through any trauma, and provide strategies tailored to your specific situation.

Forgiveness is a personal process, and it may take time. Be patient with yourself, and don't be too hard if progress seems slow. Focus on your growth and well-being and seek professional help if needed.

How to cope with life after childhood trauma as an adult.

Experienced childhood trauma. Coping with the effects of trauma can be a challenging process, but there are steps you can take to help yourself heal and move forward. Here are some strategies that may be helpful:

1. Seek professional help: Consider working with a therapist or counselor who specializes in trauma. They can provide a safe and supportive environment for you to explore your feelings, process the trauma, and develop coping mechanisms.

2. Educate yourself about trauma: Learn about the effects of trauma on the mind and body. Understanding how trauma impacts your experiences and behaviors can help you gain insight and develop strategies to manage its effects.

3. Practice self-care: Engage in activities that promote your physical, mental, and emotional well-being. This can include exercise, healthy eating, getting enough sleep, spending time in nature, practicing relaxation techniques (such as deep breathing or meditation), and pursuing hobbies and interests that bring you joy.

4. Build a support network: Surround yourself with supportive and understanding people. This may include friends, family members, support groups, or online communities. Having a network of people who can listen, offer guidance, and validate your experiences can be invaluable in the healing process.

5. Develop coping strategies: Explore healthy coping mechanisms that work for you. This might involve journaling, practicing mindfulness, engaging in creative outlets (such as art or music), or participating in activities that help you relax and recharge.

6. Set boundaries: Establish clear boundaries in your relationships and prioritize your well-being. Learning to say no and setting limits on what you're comfortable with can help you regain a sense of control and protect yourself from further harm.

7. Practice self-compassion: Be kind and patient with yourself. Recognize that healing takes time and that it's normal to have ups and downs along the way. Treat yourself with the same compassion and understanding you would offer to a loved one in a similar situation.

8. Consider support groups: Joining a support group for individuals who have experienced similar traumas can provide a sense of community, validation, and shared experiences. Hearing others' stories and sharing your own can be healing and empowering.

Everyone's journey to healing is unique, and what works for one person may not work for another. It's important to be gentle with yourself and find the strategies that resonate with you. If you find that your symptoms are significantly impacting your daily functioning, it's crucial to seek professional help.

When does the healing process start after childhood trauma?

The healing process for childhood trauma can vary significantly from person to person, and there is no fixed timeline for when it begins. The impact of childhood trauma can be long-lasting, and the healing process often involves free life addressing and working through the effects of the trauma over an extended period.

It's important to remember that healing is a highly individual journey, influenced by various factors such as the severity of the trauma, the individual's support system, their coping mechanisms, and the resources available to them.

For some individuals, the healing process may start during their childhood or adolescence as they begin to develop an understanding of what has happened to them and seek support. Others may not fully recognize or begin to address the trauma until later in life, such as during adulthood when they have gained more self-awareness and access to therapeutic resources.

It's crucial to seek professional help from therapists or counselors experienced in trauma if you or someone you know has experienced childhood trauma. These professionals can provide guidance, support, and evidence-based interventions to facilitate the healing process. Remember that healing is a gradual and non-linear process, and it can take time and effort to work through the effects of childhood trauma.

As an abused child, how do you chase the Monster away if you've experienced abuse as a child? It's important to know that I'm a language model and cannot provide real-time assistance or intervene directly in situations. However, I can offer some general advice and resources that might be helpful to you.

1. Reach out for support: It's crucial to talk to someone you trust about what you've been through. This could be a family member, friend, teacher, counselor, or a helpline specifically dedicated to supporting survivors of abuse. They can provide emotional support, and guidance, and help you explore available options.

2. Report the abuse: If you feel safe and ready, consider reporting the abuse to the appropriate authorities. Child

protective services or the police can investigate the situation and take steps to protect you from further harm.

3. Seek professional help: A mental health professional, such as a therapist or counselor, can assist you in processing your experiences, healing from the trauma, and developing coping strategies. They can also guide how to navigate the challenges you may be facing.

4. Self-care and self-compassion: Engage in activities that bring you comfort and joy. Take care of your physical and emotional well-being by getting enough rest, eating nutritious meals, and engaging in activities you enjoy. Practice self-compassion by being kind to yourself and acknowledging that the abuse was not your fault.

5. Join support groups: Connecting with others who have had similar experiences can be empowering and validating. Look for support groups or online communities where you can share your feelings, learn from others, and receive encouragement.

Everyone's situation is unique, and it's important to find the approach that feels right for you. If you're in immediate danger or experiencing a crisis, please reach out to emergency services in your country right away.

Surviving childhood trauma as an adolescent through adulthood.

Surviving childhood trauma is a challenging journey that can have long-lasting effects on individuals well into adolescence and adulthood. It is important to note that every person's experience with trauma is unique, and the impact can vary depending on various factors such as the severity of the trauma, available support systems, and individual coping mechanisms. Here are some general strategies that may help individuals in their journey of healing and recovery:

1. Seek professional help: Consider reaching out to a mental health professional such as a therapist or counselor who specializes in trauma. They can provide guidance, support, and evidence-based therapies tailored to your specific needs.

2. Build a support network: Surround yourself with trusted friends, family members, or support groups who can provide understanding, empathy, and encouragement. Sharing your experiences with others who have gone through similar situations can be immensely helpful.

3. Practice self-care: Engage in activities that promote self-care and well-being, such as exercise, mindfulness, relaxation techniques, and hobbies that bring you joy. Taking care of your physical and mental health is crucial for healing.

4. Learn coping skills: Develop healthy coping mechanisms to manage stress and emotional triggers. This may include deep breathing exercises, journaling, meditation, or engaging in creative outlets such as art or music.

5. Educate yourself about trauma: Learn about trauma and its effects to gain a better understanding of your own experiences. This knowledge can help you make sense of your emotions, reactions, and behaviors, and empower you in your healing journey.

6. Set boundaries: Establishing clear boundaries in your relationships and interactions can help protect your emotional well-being. Learning to say no and prioritize your needs is an important part of self-care.

7. Practice self-compassion: Be kind and patient with yourself as you navigate the healing process. Understand that healing from trauma takes time and effort, and it's okay to have ups and downs along the way.

8. Consider support groups: Participating in support groups or group therapy can provide a sense of community and validation. Connecting with others who have similar experiences can help reduce feelings of isolation and provide additional perspectives on healing.

9. Explore therapeutic modalities: Different therapeutic approaches may be beneficial in healing from trauma, such as cognitive-behavioral therapy (CBT), eye movement desensitization and reprocessing (EMDR), or somatic experiencing. Discuss with a mental health professional which approach may be most suitable for you.

10. Practice self-advocacy: Advocate for your needs and rights. Communicate your boundaries, seek the necessary resources, and actively participate in your healing process.

Most problematic relationships stem from childhood trauma that never was addressed.

And here's why, Childhood trauma can have a significant impact on an individual's relationships throughout their life. Unresolved childhood trauma can manifest in a variety of ways and can certainly contribute to problematic relationships. Here are a few reasons why this might be the case:

1. Attachment Issues: Childhood trauma can disrupt the development of secure attachments with caregivers. This can result in difficulties in forming healthy and trusting relationships in adulthood. Individuals may struggle

with issues such as fear of abandonment, difficulty with emotional intimacy, or an inability to trust others.

2. Emotional Regulation: Unresolved trauma can make it challenging for individuals to regulate their emotions effectively. They may experience intense emotional reactions or have difficulty healthily expressing their feelings. This can create conflicts and misunderstandings within relationships, as well as contribute to patterns of emotional reactivity or withdrawal.

3. Boundaries and Trust: Trauma can affect an individual's ability to establish and maintain appropriate boundaries in relationships. They may have difficulty setting and enforcing boundaries, leading to codependent or enmeshed dynamics. Trust issues can also emerge, making it challenging to trust others or believe in the reliability of their partners.

4. Communication Patterns: Childhood trauma can impact an individual's communication skills. They may struggle with assertiveness, struggle to express their needs and desires or have difficulty understanding and empathizing with their partner's perspective. These communication challenges can lead to misunderstandings, conflicts, and an inability to resolve relationship issues effectively.

5. Repetition of Patterns: Without addressing childhood trauma, individuals may unconsciously repeat familiar relationship patterns from their past. They may seek out partners who replicate the dynamics of their early relationships, even if those dynamics are unhealthy or abusive. This repetition can perpetuate the cycle of problematic relationships.

Addressing childhood trauma through therapy or other healing modalities can be crucial in breaking these patterns and establishing healthier relationships. Therapy can help individuals process their past traumas, develop healthier coping strategies, improve communication skills, and work towards building secure attachments and boundaries. It is important to note that addressing childhood trauma is a complex and individualized process, and it may take time and effort to heal and form healthier relationship dynamics.

Surviving the psychological aspects of childhood trauma.

Surviving the psychological aspects of childhood trauma can be a challenging and complex process, but with appropriate support and coping strategies, it is possible to heal and lead a fulfilling life. Here are some steps that may be helpful:

1. Recognize and acknowledge the trauma: Acknowledge that you have experienced trauma and understand that it is not your fault. Acceptance is an important step towards healing.

2. Seek professional help: Consider working with a mental health professional, such as a therapist or counselor, who specializes in trauma. They can provide guidance, support, and evidence-based therapies to help you process and heal from the trauma.

3. Build a support network: Surround yourself with supportive and understanding people who can provide emotional support. This can include friends, family, support groups, or online communities of individuals who have experienced similar traumas.

4. Practice self-care: Engage in activities that promote self-care and well-being. This can include exercise, mindfulness or meditation, engaging in hobbies, spending time in nature,

or pursuing creative outlets. Take care of your physical health by eating well, getting enough sleep, and avoiding substances that may negatively impact your well-being.

5. Develop coping strategies: Learn healthy coping mechanisms to manage distressing emotions and triggers associated with the trauma. This may include deep breathing exercises, grounding techniques, journaling, or engaging in relaxation techniques.

6. Educate yourself about trauma: Educate yourself about the psychological aspects of trauma and its effects. This knowledge can help you understand your experiences and develop insights into the healing process.

7. Challenge negative beliefs: Childhood trauma can lead to negative self-beliefs, such as feeling unworthy or unlovable. Work with a therapist to identify and challenge these beliefs, replacing them with positive and empowering thoughts.

8. Practice self-compassion: Be kind and compassionate towards yourself. Understand that healing takes time, and it's okay to have setbacks along the way. Treat yourself with the same care and understanding you would offer to a dear friend.

9. Engage in trauma-focused therapies: Therapies such as Eye Movement Desensitization and Reprocessing (EMDR), Cognitive-Behavioral Therapy (CBT), or Trauma-Focused Cognitive Behavioral Therapy (TF-CBT) can be effective in processing and resolving traumatic memories.

10. Maintain a healthy lifestyle: Engaging in a healthy lifestyle can support your overall well-being and aid in the healing

process. This includes maintaining a balanced diet, getting regular exercise, and practicing good sleep hygiene.

Healing from childhood trauma is a personal journey, and it may take time. Be patient with yourself and celebrate small victories along the way.

How to deal with your children after suffering from childhood trauma.

Dealing with children who have experienced childhood trauma requires patience, understanding, and a supportive environment. Here are some suggestions on how to support and help children who have suffered from trauma:

1. Educate yourself: Learn about the effects of childhood trauma and how it can impact a child's development and behavior. Understanding the underlying issues will help you respond appropriately.

2. Create a safe and stable environment: Children who have experienced trauma often need a sense of safety and predictability. Establish consistent routines, clear boundaries, and a supportive atmosphere at home. Make sure they have a safe space where they can retreat when they feel overwhelmed.

3. Be patient and empathetic: Trauma can affect a child's emotions, behavior, and ability to trust others. Be patient with their reactions and emotions, and show empathy by validating their feelings. Let them know that you are there to support them unconditionally.

4. Foster open communication: Encourage your child to express their thoughts and feelings openly, but don't force

them to share if they're not ready. Create a non-judgmental and supportive environment where they feel comfortable talking about their experiences.

5. Seek professional help: Consider involving a mental health professional who specializes in trauma if your child's symptoms persist or worsen over time. A therapist can provide specialized support and interventions to help your child heal.

6. Establish a predictable routine: Children who have experienced trauma often benefit from a structured routine. Set regular mealtimes, bedtimes, and schedules for activities and homework. Predictability can help them feel more secure and in control.

7. Encourage healthy coping mechanisms: Teach your child healthy ways to cope with stress and regulate their emotions. This could include engaging in physical activity, practicing deep breathing exercises, journaling, or engaging in creative outlets such as drawing or playing music.

8. Build a support network: Encourage your child to connect with others who have had similar experiences, such as support groups or counseling programs. Additionally, ensure they have positive role models and healthy relationships with trusted adults, such as family members, teachers, or mentors.

9. Practice self-care: Taking care of yourself is essential to provide the support your child needs. Seek your support through therapy or support groups if necessary. Practice self-care activities that help you manage stress and maintain your well-being.

The scarring effects of childhood trauma.

Childhood trauma can have significant and long-lasting effects on individuals, often referred to as "scarring effects." These effects can manifest in various areas of a person's life, including their physical, emotional, and psychological well-being. Here are some common scarring effects of childhood trauma:

1. Emotional and psychological impact: Childhood trauma can lead to a range of emotional and psychological difficulties, such as an increased risk of developing anxiety disorders, depression, post-traumatic stress disorder (PTSD), and other mental health conditions. Trauma can also affect one's self-esteem, self-worth, and ability to trust others.

2. Social and interpersonal difficulties: Children who experience trauma may struggle with forming and maintaining healthy relationships. They may have difficulty with trust, intimacy, and establishing secure attachments. These challenges can persist into adulthood, affecting romantic relationships, friendships, and overall social functioning.

3. Cognitive effects: Trauma can impact cognitive development and the ability to learn. Children who have experienced trauma may have difficulties with attention, concentration, memory, and problem-solving skills. This can have long-term consequences for academic and professional success.

4. Physical health consequences: Childhood trauma has been linked to various physical health problems later in life. Individuals who have experienced trauma may be at a higher risk of developing chronic health conditions, such as heart disease, obesity, diabetes, and autoimmune disorders. This

may be due to the physiological effects of chronic stress on the body.

5. Behavioral patterns: Childhood trauma can contribute to the development of maladaptive coping mechanisms and unhealthy behaviors. These may include substance abuse, self-harm, aggression, risky sexual behavior, and eating disorders. These behaviors can be attempts to regulate emotional pain or regain a sense of control.

6. Intergenerational transmission: Trauma can be transmitted across generations. Individuals who have experienced childhood trauma may be more likely to have difficulties in parenting, potentially perpetuating the cycle of trauma within their own families.

It's important to note that while childhood trauma can have profound and long-lasting effects, individuals are not defined solely by their past experiences. With appropriate support, therapy, and resources, people can heal, build resilience, and lead fulfilling lives.

What does life feel like after surviving Childhood trauma.

Life after surviving childhood trauma can vary greatly from person to person. It's important to note that everyone's experience is unique, and individuals may have different ways of coping and healing. However, here are some common aspects that survivors may experience:

1. Healing and Recovery: Survivors of childhood trauma often embark on a journey of healing and recovery. This process can involve therapy, counseling, support groups, or other forms of professional help. Over time, survivors may develop healthy coping mechanisms, gain a better understanding of their trauma, and work towards building a fulfilling life.

2. Emotional Challenges: Childhood trauma can have long-lasting emotional effects. Survivors may experience a range of emotions, including anxiety, depression, anger, fear, shame, guilt, or a sense of numbness. These emotions can be triggered by various factors and may require ongoing self-care and support.

3. Building Resilience: Many survivors of childhood trauma develop remarkable resilience and strength. Having survived difficult experiences, they often develop a deep understanding of their own internal resources and find ways to navigate challenges effectively. This resilience can serve as a foundation for personal growth and the ability to overcome future obstacles.

4. Positive Relationships: Childhood trauma can impact an individual's ability to form and maintain healthy relationships. Survivors may face challenges with trust, vulnerability, and intimacy. However, with healing and support, many survivors are able to establish positive and fulfilling connections with others.

5. Post-Traumatic Growth: While trauma is undoubtedly devastating, some survivors may experience post-traumatic growth. This term refers to positive changes that occur as a result of the struggle with trauma. Survivors may develop a greater appreciation for life, stronger personal relationships, a deeper sense of purpose, increased empathy, or a desire to help others who have experienced similar hardships.

6. Triggers and Flashbacks: Survivors of childhood trauma may encounter triggers—external stimuli or situations that remind them of their traumatic experiences. These triggers can evoke intense emotional and physical reactions,

sometimes leading to flashbacks—vivid re-experiences of the trauma. Learning to manage and cope with triggers and flashbacks is an important part of the healing process.

7. Self-Care and Self-Compassion: Survivors often learn the importance of self-care and self-compassion. Engaging in activities that promote physical, emotional, and mental well-being becomes crucial. This can include things like exercise, mindfulness techniques, creative outlets, self-reflection, and setting boundaries to protect oneself from further harm.

It's important to remember that healing is a nonlinear process, and individuals may have ups and downs along the way. Seeking professional support and connecting with other survivors can be beneficial in navigating the challenges and finding a meaningful life after childhood trauma.

Remember that healing from childhood trauma is a journey, and it takes time. Each child is unique, so tailor your approach to their specific needs. Providing a safe and nurturing environment, along with professional support, can significantly contribute to their recovery and resilience.

Dear son, I call him "Papa"

I hope this letter finds you well, my precious little boy. As I sit down to write these words, I am filled with overwhelming love and joy, knowing that you are a part of my life. You may not understand the depth of my feelings right now, but I want you to know how much you mean to me and how proud I am to be your dad.

From the moment you came into this world, you changed my life in ways I could never have imagined.

Your innocence, your laughter, and your endless curiosity bring light into every moment we share. Watching you grow and develop, witnessing your first steps, and hearing your first words, has been the most incredible experience of my life.

You are only two years old, yet you have already taught me so much. Your fearlessness in exploring the world around you inspires me to embrace every opportunity that comes my way. Your resilience in the face of challenges reminds me to never give up, no matter how difficult things may seem. Your unconditional love and trust have shown me the true meaning of family and the importance of cherishing every precious moment we have together.

As your dad, my role is to guide you, protect you, and be there for you every step of the way. I promise to be your rock, your confidant, and your biggest supporter. I will celebrate your successes, comfort you in times of sadness, and encourage you to pursue your dreams no matter where they may lead.

There will be times when life gets tough, my little one. There will be obstacles and setbacks along the way. But always remember that you are never alone. I am here to hold your hand and help you through any challenges that come your way. Together, we will navigate the highs and lows of life, and I will do everything in my power to ensure that you have a happy and fulfilling journey. Just like the time when you were a preemie and I used to sing to you and pray with you, I was your first nurture and I fed you and

I love you and that's the way it will be for the rest of our lives in the name of the high I pray.

I want you to know that I believe in you, my son. You have unlimited potential, and I cannot wait to see the amazing person you will become. Your kind heart, your curiosity, and your beautiful spirit will touch the lives of many, just as they have touched mine.

As the days turn into months and the months into years, know that my love for you will only grow stronger. You are the greatest gift I have ever received in life, and I am eternally grateful to have you as my son. Thank you for bringing so much love, laughter, and happiness into my life.

I also wanted you to know the love that I have for you I never got from my parents and I will never put you through the trials and tribulations that Went through a child... I never thought that I would love someone more than I love myself but you and your sister take me to a whole Other level as being a loving parent and a father thank you so very much. I'm looking so very forward to watching you and your sister grow I know you will make me proud.

So with that said, happy birthday boy.

With all my love,
Your Dad

www.ingramcontent.com/pod-product-compliance
Lightning Source LLC
Chambersburg PA
CBHW031239120626
46545CB00003B/1192